A Message from the Deacon

YOU CAN KNOW GOD TOO

Marcus D Fanning

A MESSAGE FROM THE DEACON

YOU CAN KNOW GOD TOO

MARCUS D. FANNING

P.O. BOX
VIRGINIA BEACH, VIRGINIA
WWW.FANNING-APC.COM

ISBN: 978-0615852317
Copyright © 2013 by Marcus D. Fanning
ALL RIGHTS RESERVED

PUBLISHED BY
GOODSON PUBLISHING

Acknowledgments

I would like to thank my wife Dr. LaConda Ambrose Fanning for supporting me during the process of developing A MESSAGE FROM THE DEACON. LaConda your constant encouragement and belief in this project has made this book a reality for us and I am truly grateful to you and thank God for placing you in my life. I would also like to thank my mother, Verna Fanning and my father, Marcellus Fanning, along with my brother, Maurice Fanning , Adrian, and Lula Belle Childs, my grandparents, and my children, Terry Glover, Quame Glover, and my baby girl, Logan Fanning. I would also like to thank my second mom, Ruby Brooks, and my Bishop Sidney Lee Davis. You all have been a blessing to me for lending me your lives so I could not only watch God working in my life but I have had the privilege of watching God work in your lives as well. You all provided me with inspiration for the completion of this book in one way or the other. God bless you all.

Preface

Knowledge is the ability to retain information while understanding requires logic, reasoning and application. Many people appear to gain insight but lack understanding. Let me explain, many people when asked about religion would attest to knowing God but…demonstrating a superficial level of life application or transformation.

An understanding of God is enmeshed into the fiber of our being. Change will and must occur. If this is the case one must ask do we look, act or mirror the character of God. Unfortunately, many will not apply an intentional pursuit of seeking God with a desire to understand His existence as life's crisis management plan.

Many will apply this simplistic infantile thinking to the complex dynamics of life never differentiating life from living, like from love, joy from happiness or peace from quiet. Today, there is a need to know God! There is a need to understand the significance of his relevance on this journey. Hopefully these simple messages of life will create a thirst to see the beauty of His presence and the emergent need to get to know God.

Introduction

As a youth I remember being told about God and believed in God but did not really know or understand his presence in my life. I just took the word of adults around me as truth and thought no more about it. Today I know better and as I often reflect and look back over my life I can see God in the midst of my days as a youth. I look back on my life now as if I'm watching a movie and I not only watch me growing through life, but I watch God walking with me through my life. I am always amazed at the way I missed God's presence in my past state of living. Today is a new day and I am presently aware of the presence of God in my everyday life. I see God moving and working on a daily basis and it is my deepest wish that all who read this book will be able to do the same. When you begin to watch God working and moving in your life you will begin to want to know God on a personal level. When you begin to know God you will begin to feel God on the inside of you. May God's blessings be with you all.

The Late Bloomer

On the way to bible study one evening I passed a billboard as I came off the interstate. The sign read, *Begin with the end in mind*. I thought to myself, what wonderful messages for people to see. Not long after reading the sign my wife tells me a friend of the family found out she had two weeks to live, and she wanted our pastor to visit her in the hospital so she could give her life to Christ. The first thought that came to mind was of the billboard that read *Begin with the end in mind*. This is not an isolated case. There are millions of people who believe they have time to come to the Lord, but the time is now. As you read this book you may want to know, how do I begin with the end in mind? The answer is found in the Bible.

Matthew 6:33 reads, "But seek first the kingdom of God and his righteousness…." Often time's people don't understand the importance of seeking the Lord, so they begin to get on the low road, the high road the fashion road, the clubbing road, the immorality road etc. But all roads lead to God. You may exit off the road to righteousness but you can exit onto the road of righteousness as well. The road to righteousness looks long, so being the humans we are we begin to look for shorter roads. But Matthew 3:2 says "Repent for the Kingdom of heaven is near." Don't be a late bloomer!

Realization is nothing without knowing

Imagine for a moment you're a doctor working with A.I.D.S. patients for the past twenty years. You recognize patients' symptoms before they do. Naturally it is assumed that you know everything there is about having A.I.D.S. because of your long history of working with A.I.D.S. patients. Now, what would you say if I told you that you know nothing about having A.I.D.S.? You would probably think I was crazy. The point is unless you have the virus growing within your own body, you can't know everything there is to know about having A.I.D.S.; you can only realize how bad and serious the situation is. This is why realization is nothing without knowing. Do you *know* God? Do you know what it's like to have the Spirit of the Lord growing inside your body? Or are you like many others who *realize* God exist but don't try to gain a personal relationship with him. You know the type. They make comments like, "I need to go to church one of these days" or "I know I shouldn't be living the way I am but I'll repent sooner or later" or, "You may say I can't stop drinking, doing drugs, or sleeping around and if I go to church I'll have to give it all up." Yes you have to give up worldly pleasures in exchange for Godly pleasures, and the first step is to except Jesus Christ. Christ made the ultimate sacrifice and because of this, Ephesians 3:12 tells us we are able to step into the presence of the Lord with freedom and confidence. How awesome is that? Think about it after all your mess after all your sinning after all your hell raising, God is saying don't be ashamed because you're a new man and you're a new woman and I'm not going to tear you down for past transgression but build you up in my authority. Isaiah 53:12 reads, "The God of Israel will be your rear guard…." To put into plain English, God has our backs. Now realize the seriousness of this; you have to accept Christ in order to step into the Lord's presence with freedom and confidence. I challenge you to get to know God!

Chance after Chance

God has a plan for all of us. There are always those Christians who continue to rededicate their lives to Christ. These people know that our God is a forgiving God. In Matthew 18:21-22 when the question was asked by Peter "How many times shall my brother be forgiven? Up to seven?" Jesus said, "I tell you not seven times but seventy seven times." We all know how difficult it is to forgive but Jesus tells us we must forgive from the heart because that's what God does for us. My pastor tells us we all fall but we have to learn to limit our falls. The reason is because tomorrow is not promised. You may plan to repent tomorrow when you get to church for the seventy seventh time but today you have a heart attack and die. Think about it. You fell from the word of God, you were clubbing again, fornicating again, and getting high on drugs again. Now you're dead. Maybe you have never come to know God and you would like the opportunity but now you can't even ask for another chance. If this is the case then the time is now. Don't be a late bloomer. Remember after you realize whom God is you have to know who God is. This is not Burger King; you can't have it your way when it comes to your spiritual life. God will continue to grant you chances of forgiveness as long as you occupy your body, but you have to occupy your body. Remember our physical body is just a shell that houses who we truly are. Don't fumble your life away. Get right and stay right with God before you take your last breath. If you are ready, say this prayer with me.

Dear God: *thank you for allowing me to step into your presence once again. Thank you for showing me how merciful you can be, Lord. Dear God, I understand now that I don't have to wait until tomorrow to ask for your forgiveness but I can ask right now, and I am asking you Lord to help me to make better decision in my life personally and spiritually.*

There is a Fight Going On

When I was a youth my friends and I played a game called chin checking. The object of this game was to hit each other in the chin while the person getting hit wasn't looking. We also would wrestle or box each other. The reasoning behind all of this was we wanted to be ready in case a real fight broke out. Plus, it was just funny seeing someone take a hit on the chin. Now, understand our reasoning was of the devil. **James 1:22 reads "Do not merely listen to the word, <u>and so deceive yourselves.</u>** Do what it says." Basically, what's being said is deception will come if your reasoning is not of God. That's what it's like to have reasoning out of the will of Gods. When we should have been concentrating on God and having peace in our lives we concentrated on hurting each other so we would be prepared to hurt someone else. I will say this, I would rather have a physical butt whopping than a spiritual one. Life is hitting you right now and if you're not careful, you'll get the knock out blow. You have to realize there is a spiritual fight going on and if you can't see it, then the devil already has your number<u>. Ephesians 6:10 says, "finally be strong in the Lord and all his mighty power. Ephesians 6:11 says, "Put on the full armor of god so that you can take your stand against the devil's schemes"</u> You may have a situation attacking you at this very moment: finances, setbacks, adultery, and addiction, etc. If someone were to tell me adultery is attacking their relationship with their spouse, I wouldn't be surprised. This is where you open your eyes to the spiritual fight happening everyday in households around the world. Maybe you don't mind your spouse watching pornographic movies or maybe you don't mind your spouse watching music videos with half naked women dancing with their chest and butts out. Maybe you don't mind going out to see a movie titled Booty Call. Maybe you don't mind getting dressed and looking sexy so you can go to the night club with your spouse, so he can see all the other women who got dressed and are looking sexy also. Or maybe you don't mind if your spouse goes to the strip club as long as he comes home to you. Please understand the devil using the I don't mind or I don't care attitude as fuel for adultery. This is just one example of the devil's tricks. For the purpose of this book the adulterer was a man, but could have easily been a woman. When you are constantly bombarded with relaxed attitudes about sex, promiscuity will happen. ___**We cannot allow loosened standards to justify our flesh!**___ Please remember *there is a fight going on* and we are all in the middle of it. *Don't be a late bloomer.* Realize that *you have to know who God is* in your life.

Blaming Others for an Undisciplined Life

Proverbs 5:23 says, "He will die for lack of discipline." Have you ever noticed when someone cheats in a relationship that the person doing the cheating blames the person being cheated on. The other person is always to blame when the cheater is the one who wasn't strong enough to say no. The other person is to blame when the cheater didn't set appropriate boundaries.

Our maybe you know someone who loves their significant other when the finances are good but hates them when their financial situation is sub-par. Or it's your mates fault when you weren't disciplined with your finances; you wanted top of the line products on a bottom of the line budget. Proverbs 13:18 says, **"He who ignores discipline comes to poverty."**… I know of a young man who blamed his mother for ruining his relationship with his girlfriend because the mother would not allow the young girl to spend the night in his room. **Proverbs 18:19 says, "discipline your son, for in that there is hope; do not be a willing party to his death"**…. I say if having a morally disciplined life style is wrong then I don't want to be right. **Proverbs 10:17 says "He who heeds discipline shows the way to life".**… There comes a time when we must be responsible for our actions and stop blaming others for our selfish undisciplined out of the will of God actions. *Don't be a late bloomer know who God* is in your life.

Life's Turns

While in the Navy I learned the difference in the way a car turns and the way a ship turns. Cars make a sharper turn, while ships have a tendency to slide when they turn. In life people turn just like ships. Understand that ships look for and turn at markers. These markers maybe water buoys, lighthouses, or a host of different things. As people we turn at markers also, no not ocean markers but at life's markers. Some of us turn at bottles and begin to slide into alcoholism. The devil is the master of confusion. He will have you thinking your turning at the crack of dawn, but it's really a crack pipe and you slide into drug addiction. Then there are the bold ones that say let's turn at the sin marker, and when they do they slide right into destruction. Gods' word is telling us that we don't have to continue turning at the wrong marker in our lives. God has provided us with some navigational rules to help us navigate safely along the seas of our lives. Now, if you have been making the wrong turns in your life and you want to make the right turns do what the Lord says. First of all slow down before you get to your marker. Then, begin to make your turn early so that when you slide you slide into position. If you turn correctly, your first turn should be toward our Lord and Savior Jesus Christ. Matthew 8:26 says **<u>Jesus got up and rebuked the winds and the waves and it was completely calm</u>.**" Continue to turn and slide into position your next turn may be toward your pastor for spiritual guidance. If you want to know how to get a hold of these rules, look no further than your bible. This is where you learn to navigate the rough seas of your life, and begin to make the right turn. Soon, even when the seas get rough there will be smooth sailing for you, because Jesus can calm your seas. You won't have to turn anymore; you can sail straight home where the Lord will be waiting. Remember to slow down and turn early. Don't be a late bloomer.

Dear God, *help me to navigate the rough seas in my life. I come to you with a humble heart yielding to your will Lord, because I believe only you can order my steps and bring me the joy and peace I've been searching for. Amen.*

Dashboard Knees

Early in our marriage while still in the Navy my wife had a car accident, she was hit by and eighteen wheeler. The big diesel truck hit my wife's car and she spun out of control and hit the divider walls on highway. My wife's left knee was banged up from crashing into the wall. She had gone through physical therapy for a while until her leg was better and she was able to walk on it again. Twenty years later you would never know something was wrong with her knee at all. You would never know something was wrong with her knee until she begins to rub alcohol it. Even though the day she was in that terrible accident is a distant memory from her past she still has a reminder from time to time. I would say at least three times a year for maybe a week I'll see her nursing the leg rubbing it down with alcohol and taking a Tylenol to ease the pain she fills at that moment. During these few times a year when she is nursing her knee her normal activities don't stop she just deals with a reminder of her past until the pain subsides. I think about her knee often because it reminds me of the way life is. People have to deal with all types of issues and tragedies and personal setbacks which have a tendency to make us hurt and feel pain. As people of God we need to understand that the worst is already over. The pain, heartache, depression, guilt, and anger you feel is just a reminder of where you came from and the things you've had to endure and overcome in your past. It is important to *Get to know who God is in your life.*

Dear heavenly father we come know thanking you for every trial and tribulation we've endured during the course of our lives. Lord we say thank you because we are still standing we have not been defeated, because you have been with us even in our dark

17

places in life. Dear God we give you praise and honor because our momentary pain is just a reminder of how far we have come with you by our side. Amen

Who Are You Leading?

When Moses came down from Mt.Sinai he said to Aaron, **Exodus 33:21 <u>"What did these people do to you, that you led them into such great sin?"</u>** Almost three thousand people died that day, because of Aaron's if you can't beat them join them attitude. Aaron tried to befriend the people by pleasing them, but what the people needed was a leader. Parents listen when I say our children will have plenty of friends, but they need parents who will lead when leadership is needed; not please when leadership is needed. The effects of Aaron's bad leadership were death. **The effects of bad parenting are death.** As a child I wanted to please my parents like most children do, and liked to learn but became discouraged. I would ask for assistance with my homework from my father but, my father's idea of helping and motivating me was to pluck me in the middle of my forehead and call me stupid. He would encourage me to ask questions, but by the fourth grade I was discouraged because I was tired of being yelled at and plucked in the head every time I asked questions and didn't understand a lesson. I began to withdraw, and when I needed help my father who was the leader in my life was the last person I would ask. I began to become afraid of ridicule at school and at home. The love of learning began to die. I know a mother who encouraged her son to be the best basketball player he could be. This kid could really play and his mother made sure he played as much as he wanted. This young man would be on three teams at a time. Well, his mother should have left some time for school because at 20 years old he is depressed and left without a high school diploma, or GED. **<u>Hosea 4:6 reads "My people are destroyed for lack of knowledge."</u>** As the leader in his life she must understand she is able to give him more than a basketball. He can become many positive things. Now is the time to bring this young man into the knowledge of the Lord. It's not too late to have God breathe life into his situation. I have a question for the parents, but it's also for the pastors, deacons, aunts, uncles, brothers, sisters, cousins, etc. **who** are you leading? **<u>Proverbs 11:14 says, "For lack of guidance a nation falls."</u>** Dear parents and leaders please get to know who you are in God. It's not too late.

Dear God, *I humbly come before you asking you to help me become the leader you would have me to be God. I gladly accept the responsibility of being a servant in your kingdom. Lord allow me to be an example for others to follow in Jesus name I pray amen.*

Philippians 4:19 "And my God will meet all your needs"… Our needs have been met; the problem is that we don't think they have. I remember reading the book "Up From Slavery" by Booker T. Washington. In the book Mr. Washington spoke of families who lived in the plantation districts. Their common diet was fat pork and cornbread, which was bought at high prices. But as Booker T. Washington evaluated the situation, he began to realize there was enough land for them to plant vegetable gardens. Mr. Washington said, "Their one objective -seemed to be to plant cotton, and in many cases cotton was planted up to the very door of the cabin." I can only imagine the possibilities of what would have happened if just one of the families began to plant a garden while growing cotton. Maybe their meals would have been healthier. Maybe some money was to be made from the sale of the produce. Mr. Washington could see what God had provided those families, and it was his duty to help them see it. How many of us waste what God has provided daily? The opportunity to get educated is wasted. The opportunity to become employed is wasted. The opportunity to start businesses is wasted. But most of all, the opportunity to get to know God is wasted. *The distractions of the world have a way of making people waste what God has put in front of them.* Isaiah 58:11 " **The Lord will guide you always; he will satisfy your needs in the sun-scorched land and will strengthen your frame"….** God is everywhere and he wants us all to see the blessings he has laid before us. You don't have to be a late bloomer, you don't have to waste another moment getting to know God.

A Snake's Tale

As a youth I had a real fear of snakes. This one day I was waiting for my mother. We had some errands to run. While waiting in our yard I noticed a large snake sitting beside my foot. I wanted to run but my legs were stuck. I was frozen and couldn't move. I called to my mother, what's wrong she says? With a shaky voice I said, "It's a snake by my leg". My mother reached out her hand to me a said, "Come on". I answered, "I can't move my legs". My mother then grabs my arm and says, "Come on I got you". My legs began to move; they were moving stiffly but moving. The lesson is that God is reaching out to us. Continually he is saying take my hand, I'm here for you. Only God can deliver us for our fears.   Not long after that incident I had a similar occurrence of events. This time I was with my grandfather. We were going fishing. While walking to the lake I spotted a couple of snakes. I froze again and said, "Grandpa, I see snakes." My Grandfather turned and looked at the snakes and said, "You better come on they won't bother you". He kept walking. Immediately my legs began to move, I ran to his side and walked the rest of the way to the lake stride for stride with him. I had to make a decision there was no time to be scared because he wasn't waiting for me. When it comes to God the time to make a decision is now. Just because we are supposed to wait on the Lord doesn't mean he has to wait on us. We as Christians must say Lord I choose to walk stride for stride with you today. At that time of my life I knew very little about snakes; I know now the snake in my yard was not poisonous. But I was petrified just the same. **<u>Psalm34: 4 "I sought the Lord he answered me; he delivered me from all my fears".</u>** There was no need for me to be afraid. I could have taken steps but fear stopped me. What is stopping you from taking the steps you need to take toward God? I know now the snakes by the lake were poisonous, but I did not allow fear to consume me in that situation. I decided to not just walk with my Grandfather but be obedient also. He told me to

come on and I immediately followed. When are Christians going to start being obedient to God and walking with God instead of away from him?

Walking in Authority

As a child a woman named Ruby kept me while my mother worked. My grandmother would say, "She thinks she your momma; she has you on her hip all the time". This was true because if Ruby wasn't carrying me I was holding on to her. She had seven children of her own, so I was an extension to the family. This one day everyone seemed to be home having a good time. While we were talking and enjoying each other's company on Ruby's porch we heard sirens and a screeching sound. The noise was coming from the street corner. There was another family who stayed further up the street and the policemen were chasing them. The teenagers began to jump out of the car and run home. They lived on the opposite corner so they had to run past Ruby's house to get home. Ruby came off her porch and told everyone to stay still where he or she was. But I was attached to her hip so when she moved I moved. She walked to where the edge of her yard meets the sidewalk. When she got to the sidewalk those other children came running past her, all but one. By this time the police have positioned themselves and had drawn their guns. Then one of Ruby's children says "Momma you and Marcus better get back up here". Ruby calmly looks back at me then she pulls me behind her back and says, **"I'll never let you all stand in the face of danger".** The last person to get out of the car is approaching fast and he had his gun drawn. I looked through the open space between Ruby's arm and the young man looked as if he was going to turn and shoot at the police. Keep in mind this is happening really fast, as he gets closer he looks Ruby in her eye and she looks him in his eye and begins to shake her head no and suddenly he puts the gun into his pants runs past Ruby and runs home. **Mark 1:25-26 says "Be quiet!" said Jesus sternly. "Come out of him!" The evil spirit shook the man violently and came out of him with a shriek.** I can't say if Ruby pulled an evil spirit out of the young man that day, but I believe she definitely backed that evil spirit down. I think of that day often, she did three key things I want everyone to notice. 1) She did not hesitate to <u>sacrifice herself</u>. That's why she came off the porch and told everyone to stay still. Understand if anything was going to happen it was going to happen to her and not her children. 2) She became a <u>protector</u> when she pulled me behind her back. The gunman could have easily grabbed her or a bullet could have hit her. The point is whatever happened she was going to get it before me. I wasn't her biological child but she protected me as if I was. 3) She, as I see it, became the gunman's <u>conscience.</u> When she looked him in his eye and shook her head no, she saved his life. She walked in the authority of her motherhood not only with her children but also with the gunman and me. She didn't have to call my mother and ask if it was ok to be a body shield for me. In those few short minutes she touched the lives of three families; hers plus two more. She walked in a mother's authority because she had a personal relationship with God. She knew no matter what happened everything was going to be all right. This is because God granted her authority. **1Corinthians 11:10 "the woman ought to have a sign of authority on her head…."**Ruby's attitude was, God if it's my time to come home I'm coming without hesitation. **Mathew 10:28 "Do not be afraid of those who kill the body but cannot kill the soul…."**. Some may say she would have left this world and her children would've been without a mother. But I remember that day and in the face of danger when my mother was not there I still had a mother, when the gunman's mother wasn't there he still had a mother. We don't know when how or where God is going to use someone, but I know he used her that day. Get to know God. It's not too late. Salvation is yours.

Let Your Burdens Go

I was watching some show on animals a few years ago and it really touched me. There was this man setting a trap for a baboon he dropped a salt cube in a hole and walked away. As the trapper was walking away a baboon approached the hole and stuck his hand inside. The baboon grabbed the salt cube but could not pull his hand out of the hole, because his hand was now made into a fist. With the baboon's hand bald up the way it was it became impossible for the animal to pull his hand out. There is panic on the animal's face but it gets worse. When it turns around and sees the trapper returning to the hole. The man was not returning empty handed either he had a cage in his hand. <u>Keep in mind there is nothing but open space for the baboon to run to,</u> as the trapper slowly returns to the hole. The baboon's dilemma was easy to solve. All he had to do was let the salt cube go and he could've pulled his hand out of the hole. Finally the animal released the salt but it was too late, because the trapper had successfully captured the baboon. The baboon did not let go until he was in the cage and the situation was worse than the previous one. You may be wondering why I'm telling this story; well the answer is this. The salt cube was representation of a burden. We all have them or have had them or will have them. Burdens have a way of stressing us out and not allowing us to see the bigger picture. The man setting the trap was a representation of the devil. The devil sets the initial traps in our lives then he allows us to trap ourselves by not taking the opportunities of escape provided by God. The cage was representation of a coffin. As Christians we like to say it's never too late to come to Christ but when the coffin closes if the decision wasn't made before hand then it's too late. Psalms 55:22 "**Give your burdens to the Lord and he will take care of you….**" The open space was a representation of God. We must understand that God is everywhere in our lives and all we have to do is let go of our burdens and give them to God and everything will be all right. The baboon saw the trapper coming towards him and still refused to let the salt go. I won't say the baboon represents us humans, but I will say as humans we need to let our burdens go; especially when we see the devil getting busy in our lives. Remember to walk in the authority granted you by God and let your burdens go.

You Have to Feel the Pain before You Release

I arrived home from work one day and my wife made a request of me. The request was a simple one. All she wanted me to do was put the iron away for her. I immediately said sure no problem. Here is when things went bad. Instead of grabbing the iron by the handle I grabbed it by the base. As soon as I grabbed the iron I knew I was in trouble. I wanted to let go but I couldn't. When I grabbed the iron I had no choice but to allow the signal from my burning hand to reach my brain. I was looking with my eyes and knew I should let the iron go but I had to wait for the signal from my brain to get back to my hand and say release. This is one of those situations where explaining what happened won't do the story any justice. This is also one of those situations where you have to go through it to understand. <u>The thing I'm trying to get everyone to understand is that in order to release I had to feel the pain first.</u> Many Christians today have what is called a pharaoh attitude.

In order for the pharaoh to release the Israelites, he had to suffer some things, most notably plagues. The pharaoh went through ten different plagues before he released the Israelites and he still changed his mind. We have a tendency to hold on to things in life that we should not. This is the reason we end up getting hurt. When you hold on to the wrong things in life you will be hurt in some form or fashion. Just as I did when I held onto the Iron I wanted to let go but couldn't. People feel all the time I can't let go of this relationship, I can't let go of this man or this woman, I can't let go of these drugs or this alcohol, etc.etc. . author and life couch tony Robbins all the time "whenever you feel you can't do something then you must do something" Let Jesus have all those issues, give them to God so that you can rest in the Lord.

Cracked Shells Lead to Rotten Eggs

If I had a carton of eggs and had to choose a two year-old holding them and a twenty year-old holding them, I would choose the twenty year-old. This is a choice I believe most of us would choose. Eggs are fragile and must be handled with care. If someone were to crack an egg and let it set for a while it would begin to rot, and produce and awful smell. Just as the eggs are fragile so are the minds of our children. The cracked eggs in this case are a representation of the fragile **egos** of our children. Who do you leave the care of your children to? Is it in the care of someone who is encouraging or discouraging? We have a tendency as people to look at teenagers as if their all bad, but the truth is not that the teenagers are bad or rotten like eggs it's just that deep in their soul, a lot of them have been rotting on the inside for a long time. From the time they were toddlers they have had to deal with something. Which over time manifest in their lives and has a tendency to look bad or rotten. The parent or the person who is the so called authority figure in the lives of our children do things sometimes that crack fragile egos. When Daddy who is his son or daughters hero decides he wants to have sex with him or her he has cracked his child's ego. When momma who is super woman to her child begins to take drugs and sleep with every Tom, Dick, and Harry, well momma doesn't look so super anymore and she has cracked some fragile egos. Most parents and leaders in the children's lives have in most cases unknowingly cracked a few fragile egos. Mathew 16:6 Jesus said "Be on your guard against the yeast of the Pharisees and Sadducees."... Jesus knew how a small amount of yeast could affect the outcome of

bread. He also knew the yeast (bad teaching) of the Pharisees and Sadducees could have and evil effect on a fragile mind. Let me give you a few examples of what I'm talking about. My cousin's daycare worker used to get him to lick between her legs at the age of four. I had no idea we were both little kids so when he would come around and want to jump on every girl he saw it made me uncomfortable because we were like six or seven years old. When he should have been thinking about playing in the park with other children he was thinking about having sex with other children. His day care worker turned him on to something he truly was not prepared to handle. The book of Mark tells us that it better for you to jump into the ocean with a stone tied to your neck than introduce a child of God to sin! Listen we all have heard stories about young girls being molested at home and then blaming their selves for breaking up mommy and daddies happy home.

All hope is not lost when we crack our eggs, there are options. Eggs can be scrambled when cracked; if the crack is small enough you can still boil the egg. Some cracks are larger than others but you can still poach an egg. Let's not forget about pies, cakes, cookies, etc. The list of uses goes on and on.

If we can find a use for a cracked egg we can definitely find a use for a child whose ego has been cracked. My wife is a Christian psychologist who does great work with children; she is excellent at getting to the root of the issues confronting children today. My wife is always receiving calls from young men and women who just want to thank her for helping them find their way in this world. These young people share their testimonies and good news because when no one else believed in them, when everyone else thought these young people could do nothing but destroy everything around them Dr. LaConda Fanning was there to say "I understand your pain, and past and I believe in your future".

Saving our children begins with the word of God. Romans 10:9 "That if you confess with your mouth, "Jesus is lord," and believe in your heart that God raised him from the dead, you will be saved...." To see the manifestation of change in a person is such a glorious testament to the power of God. Those cracked egos can become anything the Lord would have them to be, how awesome is that? Bring your children before God so he can renew their minds. Moses said, in Deuteronomy 30: 19 "Now choose life so that your children may live…." The time is now don't be a late bloomer, *allow your children the opportunity to get to know God.*

Dust Grandma Dust

When I was a young man, I would visit my grandparents with my brother and one or more of my cousins. The one thing she did daily was clean her house. To the naked eye the house did not need any cleaning but she cleaned anyway. My grandmother lived in the country with my grandfather. I remember how fresh the house used to smell and she would raise the blinds and then she would raise the windows and the sun would shine through and a breeze would begin to move through the house. I can't explain how good a feeling it was being in her home.

The one burning issue she had with her home was the dust. I remember her saying "for some reason I just can't get rid of this dust". My grandmother did not want even the smallest amount to settle. It's hard keeping dust away period, but looking back I realize how hard it was to keep the dust away when she stayed on the side of the road. The cars would come by and kick up dirt and she had the windows open so some dust was going to come in. This is why she was so vigilant and could see the dust when everyone else couldn't.

You are reading and thinking what does his grandmothers' dust have to do with anything. Thinking of my grandmother in that setting reminds me of the work preachers do all the time. Well my grandmother loved her house but she did not love the dust that came with her house. Preachers love the people in their congregation but they do not love the sin that comes with the people. Ministers can see the sin even when you can't. This is what happens The Minister sends everyone home on Sunday. Now one week later the minister opens the doors and the congregation comes in for another Sunday service. Well when the congregation comes in from the world and settle in their seats they bring a little dust with them. I'm not talking about the kind my Grandmother used to see. The dust I'm talking about is sin, and the pastor has to use the word of God to clean everyone up again. If your sin is fornication, there's a word for it, if your sin is homosexuality, there's a word for it. No matter what your sin, there is a word to help clean up your life. John 15:3 Jesus said "You are already clean because of the word I have spoken in you...." But you have to keep the word in you.

Have you ever seen a young child who didn't want to take a bath? The young boy or girl may say something like I took a bath three days ago. This is the same attitude the so called saved church going person has. You may know some of these saved people; they go to church on Sunday but never attend bible study or Sunday school. They never or rarely read their bible. Please understand that Sunday is not the only opportunity there is for us to get cleaned by the word of God. Most of us take care of our physical and oral hygiene on a daily basis, so the question that must be asked is why wouldn't we do the same with our spiritual hygiene? 2 Timothy 2: 21 " If a man cleanses himself of the latter, he will be an instrument for noble purposes, made holy , and prepared to do a good work...."

Dear God I humbly come before you asking you to cleanse my soul and wash my sins away. Make me pure in your sight Lord so that I may go before you and do a good work. God allow me to not be just another spectator in your house, but allow me to be a participator in all that is of you. God I ask only that you allow me to be a blessing and a willing vessel to be used to bring the Good News forward, so that I may not only continue to keep my soul clean but I can also be used to cleanse the soul of others. Amen

.

Find the Remote Control

Do you know of anyone who lost the remote control to the television?

I will start with myself and say that I have lost the remote on a few occasions and I refused to stop looking until I found it. I also know of people who have lost the remote and reacted in the same manner that I have. People will sit on the couch all day and watch television and won't use any energy. But let the remote get lost and people will drop about ten pounds trying to figure out what happened to the remote control. Ask yourself this question especially if you have ever found yourself looking for a remote control, have you ever found yourself looking for God with the same amount of energy? Hebrews 11: 6 says "He rewards those who earnestly seek him…."

What reward has finding the TV remote ever given anyone? If you want satisfaction in your life seek the Lord.

Oh I Forgot

When my boys Terry and Quame were 7and 8 I would make sure to be home when they arrived from school. I would make sure all their homework was done and I would make sure they ate a snack and then dinner. This was the routine. My wife did not get home from work until 7pm so the only thing left to do was make sure the boys showered for the night. Well this one particular evening my wife called and she spoke with Terry, the 8 year old. Terry then hands me the phone and my wife is upset. Terry has asked her to bring something home to eat because he was hungry. Now my wife grew up very poor so to have one of her children say they were hungry would set her off.

She gets on the phone and demands to know why our kids haven't eaten yet. My response was "what are you talking about they ate dinner 45minutes ago."

My wife then says, "Well what is he talking about?" So I put Terry back on the phone and she asked "why did you tell me you didn't eat?" and his reply was "**oh I forgot**, well can you bring me some candy or a soda to drink?" Here is the thing I want everyone to catch. There are a lot of people going around with an oh I forgot state of mind. He was only 8 at the time, but what is your excuse? For 365 days a year for 18-25 years our children have been fed, clothed, loved, guided, sheltered, and disciplined. You do the math. I will put it in a nut shell; our children have been taken care of. They have been taken such good care of that they take it for granted. *They have become so used to getting that they can't remember what they just got.* It does not stop with our children this problem exists in our marriages also. Married people have a tendency to forget what one spouse has done for the other. When was the last time you just told your spouse or significant other thank you for the meal you just ate or when was the last time you said thanks for keeping our children safe and sheltered. When was the last time you even thought about how well you're being taken care of?

Well the time to think about things is now. I know of a woman who decided to leave her husband for a number of reasons. The husband did not want to lose his family. He made it known he wanted the wife and children to stay. The wife persisted and they separated for a little over a year and in that time she was able to think about the many good things he brought to the table. They ended up getting back together and she says she did not know how to appreciate her husband or family situation the way she does now.

The same is true of our children. They want to leave home when they turn 18 but they return when they get a taste of the world and realize life is a little easier at home with mom and dad. They remember how it is to not pay bills and not have responsibility beyond helping keep the house clean or taking care of their brother or sister.

Have you forgotten? I think you have. You have forgotten how good God has been to you. You have forgotten how easy it is for you to breathe, walk talk, or have the right thinking of your mind. Have you forgotten who allows your loved ones to do the same? You have a good job, Oh you forgot who gave it to you. You have a blessed life Oh you forgot who gave it to you. You found love but you forgot who gave you a heart. Well, this is what   Deuteronomy 32:18-20 says. "You forgot the God who gave you birth…."

The Lord saw this and rejected them because he was angered by his sons and daughters. "I will hide my face from them, he said, "and see what their end will be…."

What is taking your mind off God and the good things he is doing in your life. Get to know who God is in your life so you don't forget all the many blessings he has set before you.

Dear God I come asking you to keep my mind, keep my mind Lord from straying from your goodness. Lord keep my mind from straying from your blessings past, present, and future. Oh I remember Lord how you kept me in the midnight hour; I remember how you kept me when I was in my mess. Lord I remember how you kept me blessed when I couldn't see the blessing set before me. Lord I remember when you made a way out of no way, and I thank you Lord and give you all the praise. Lord I remember most of all how you gave me your holy word to keep me and guide me. All praises to you God now and forever amen.

Put It on The shelf

My wife tells me that when she was a young girl her mother used to tell her children that she was going to put it on the shelf for them. I wanted to know what she meant by that statement. My wife used her brother as an example. She said he got in trouble a lot and every time he did my wife's mother would say to her son, "I am going to put it on the shelf for you." When my wife repeated the saying I kept thinking of putting cans on a shelf. I was puzzled, but as she began to further explain I began to understand. My wife's brother repeated the wrong behavior too many times and finally he found out that it wasn't cans his momma was putting on the shelf but it was butt whippings she was putting on the shelf. Now I think it is very interesting how she put each incident on the shelf but when she finally took them off the shelf she took them off at one time. Hebrews 2:2 says "For the message God delivered through his angels has always stood firm, and every violation of the law and every act of disobedience was punished". Every act of disobedience was punished. Just imagine God putting all your sins on the shelf and one day he decides to take those sins off the shelf and punish you for each sin at one time. The time is now to get to know who God is in your life.

Do you remember when sin first entered your life? Do you remember the result of the entry of sin into your life? The answer for most people is probably no. But I am a person who remembers when he first was turned on to sin. I did not know at the time what was happening and I did not realize I was sinning either, but the person who turned me on should have known better.

I believe I was in kindergarten when I had my first lustful dream. I dreamed of laying my teacher on the table in one of the school rooms and with me on top kissing her passionately. I also was rubbing my body against hers. We both had our clothes on because I did not know more. I also realized at this time I had something below the belt. I wondered to myself why I was having this dream every time I closed my eyes. The reason is clear now; it was because of the way the teacher used to kiss me. Mark 7:21- 23 " For from within, out of men's hearts, come evil thoughts, sexual immorality, theft, murder, adultery, greed, malice, deceit, lewdness, envy, slander, arrogance and folly. All these evils come from inside and make a man unclean." She was my first French kiss or tongue kiss whatever you want to call it. She would pull me aside as a young boy and show me how to kiss. After the kisses came the fantasy of she and I or you might say a lustful spirit came over me. Innocence was lost and she took it. My friend saw this teacher kiss me and he said I wish she would kiss me like that. His innocence was lost; was he having fantasy of her also? I don't know but she sure did provide a spark. Most people think they are not doing any harm but I say this if you are leading people away from God instead of toward God you are doing harm to those people. The goal is to turn people on to God and not on to sin. My teacher thought she wasn't doing any harm. Well Hitler thought he wasn't doing any harm either. But if we ask the Jews, what would they say. All I ask is that all people take a look at themselves and evaluate the effect there having on the people they come in contact with. I especially want people to evaluate the effect we are having on children. *Don't be a late bloomer get to know who God is in your life.*

Drowning in Problems

I used to have this recurring dream where millions of other people were in the ocean struggling to keep their head above water. Everyone in the dream was treading water trying to stay afloat in the ocean. Everyone was busy trying to save themselves. There was no pulling together and no team work just each person trying to keep his or her head above water. I was one of the millions of people treading water trying to stay afloat, but then I realized something. Everyone was treading water for a long time the sun rose and fell and rose and fell again. I began to realize no one was drowning but everyone was trying to stay afloat. When I made this realization I said Lord help me and suddenly I began to see the shore and on the shore was a man in the distance. As I focused my attention on the man in the distance, the shore became closer and I was able to swim to the beach and get out of the water. I looked back to try and encourage people, but they were so fixated on their situation that they continued to tread water, and I began to go back in the water. I had to turn around and keep looking at the man in the distance. I began to notice there were others ahead of me walking toward the man in the distance. Who was the man in the distance? The man in the distance was Jesus Christ, and all everyone had to do was realize they were already saved and get out the water. **Romans 10:13 says for everyone who calls upon the name of the Lord will be saved.**

The water in my dream was a representation of the issues or sins people deal with on a daily basis, you may hear terms like I'm drowning in debt, or drowning in my sorrows, etc., etc. Don't be a late bloomer get to know who God is in your life.

The Time is Now

At the beginning of this book I wrote about a woman whose doctor said she only had two weeks to live. You have to understand that she received the news all of the sudden. This was not a countdown you have six months; now you have four months to live. Her situation was you have two weeks to live, no ifs ands or buts about it. Her husband was a truck driver he was on the road, and she had no family other than her husband in the local area. She was living in Virginia but she was originally from Texas. I want you to watch what happens. This woman who has been given two weeks to live, who had no support at the time, and is drowning in her sickness, drowning in depression, and loneliness, makes a decision. She asked her friend to see if her Pastor would come visit her so she can give her life to Christ so that she can be saved. The Pastor agrees to see this woman he has never met before and when he comes in the room he and the woman finds out they have a common bond. He noticed that she was a Dallas Cowboys fan and so was he. They began to talk and found out they weren't just fans but the both of them were from the state of Texas. Watch this. Her husband was not there and her family was not there, but in the mist of her need she found someone whom she could relate to. And just not anyone, but a man of God. This woman who has just two weeks to live has a good time and she and the Pastor go over the Plan of Salvation together so that she may be saved. The next day the doctors tell her they are not able to treat her illness and that there is only one hospital in the country that specializes in her particular illness. She wants to know where the hospital is and to her surprise it's in Texas. Dallas to be exact. Her home town A place where she can spend her last days with her loved ones, a place her and her husband call home. Let's review. She asked to give her life to Christ so that she may be saved and God stepped right in sent her a pastor who in her time of need she could relate to because they shared a common background they were both living in Virginia but were originally from Dallas Texas. Then she gave her life to Christ, and the next day's received the news she would be spending her last days in Texas with her family. Well her two weeks has turned into four years, she is alive and well living in Texas thanks be to God!! THE TIME IS NOW GET TO KNOW WHO GOD IS IN YOUR LIFE!!!!

Remember you can Know God Too!!!!!!

www.ingramcontent.com/pod-product-compliance
Lightning Source LLC
Chambersburg PA
CBHW060950050426
42337CB00052B/3434